A House Called Paddockhurst

A short history and description of Worth's Victorian mansion

By
Dom Ian Condon O.S.B.

INTRODUCTION

Worth School is fortunate to be situated in an area of outstanding natural beauty, a site of tranquillity and peace. We are also fortunate in occupying Paddockhurst House, a building whose history and evolution, like that of the school, has changed over time to meet the needs of its inhabitants. Its changes reflect the character and aspirations of its various owners. Much of the beauty and fine artistry of the house can be found in the small and often overlooked areas as well as in the grand rooms and their decoration.

Dom Ian Condon's thoughtful and well informed guide enables visitors to apprise themselves of the many hidden charms of this building and the concern for detail that was once lavished on this family home. Paddockhurst House remains a home to this day albeit for a small army of boy boarders rather than for any one particular family. It is very much an example of living history and a place of beauty that enables its current occupants to be inspired and to appreciate the connectivity of the past, present and future.

Gino Carminati

Head Master
Worth School

THE INITIATIVE OF
ABBOT JOHN CHAPMAN OF DOWNSIDE

In the early 1930s, Abbot John Chapman of St Gregory's, Downside, was looking for more adequate buildings to which to move his Junior School. With this aim in view, some 30 locations were examined before deciding on a large country house called Paddockhurst, situated on a ridge of the Sussex Weald. The house was formerly the property of the first Lord Cowdray, who had died in 1927. It lay in 500 acres of landscaped grounds surrounded by woods and fields and with a distant view southwards over rolling countryside towards Ditchling Beacon on the Downs and northwards in the direction of modern-day Gatwick airport. The land immediately around the house was included in the sale in 1933 along with farm buildings, workshops and cottages. Due to its height above sea level (184 metres) the air, though not bracing, is always very fresh.

Visitors often ask about the history of the house. What follows is an attempt to answer their questions and to give an account of this beautiful property, which used to be called Paddockhurst.

Part I

The Site and its Former Owners

In the Seventeenth and Eighteenth Centuries

The first time the name of the property called Paddockhurst occurs is in 1691 when it appears to be part of the Wakehurst estate of Ardingly. A deed of sale of that year shows that Sir William Culpeper of Wakehurst sold part of what used to be Wakehurst Park as a separate property known as Paddockhurst. Old Farm Cottages, the timber frame house in the hollow to the right of the main gate, is thought to be the oldest building, possibly fifteenth century. The right hand building up the slope to the left of the drive was the main house of the original property, or at least the site of it. Paddockhurst was originally little more than a farm house. The present house is probably late eighteenth or early nineteenth century. Between 1691 and 1862 there were a series of owners who seem to have been minor gentry.

The Victorian Age

The transformation that came over Paddockhurst reflects the new wealth that was being made in Victorian England. The great house was the creation of three self-made men, who were successively owners of Paddockhurst. The first was a London builder, whose wealth came from the population explosion. The second was an engineer, whose skills were a product of the Industrial Revolution in which Britain led the way. The third was a civil engineer and contractor when British skills were in demand all over the world.

George Smith, the Builder

In 1862, a wealthy London builder named George Smith, of Wimpole Street, London, bought Paddockhurst. He soon decided that the old house on the hill did not measure up to his expectations. Smith selected a site about 300 metres south-east of the old house and invited a well-known architect, Anthony Salvin (1799-1881), who had worked on Windsor Castle, to design a mock Tudor mansion. This was completed in 1865. The old house on the hill then became Old Paddockhurst. It is difficult to picture today the new house as it was. Although it is the nucleus of the present house, it looked very different. It was of two floors (instead of the present three) and the stables were beside the house on its north side, separated from it by only a few metres. There was a porte-cochere or drive-in porch at the front door.

The house in Smith's time with the porte-cochere

Robert Whitehead, the Inventor (1823–1905)

In 1881, Paddockhurst was sold to Robert Whitehead, a Lancashire man and marine engineer who became part of a "brain-drain" from Britain. He was a fascinating character who had known Garibaldi and had worked for the Imperial Austro-Hungarian Navy at its Adriatic base in Fiume. He was heaped with Austro-Hungarian honours and his daughters made aristocratic marriages; one of them was the first wife of the father of the von Trapp family who, many years later, were to delight the world as the Trapp Family Singers. Whitehead made a fortune as the inventor of the torpedo, the most famous model of which bears his name. Sadly, he was never honoured in his own country, where he remained plain Mr Whitehead. When he retired to Sussex in his old age, he bought Paddockhurst from Smith's executors and proceeded to make grandiose changes.

In 1883 the huge Music Room was added on the south-west corner of the house, extending the south garden front. The wing was designed by Sir Arthur Cawston (a well-known architect of the time, who died tragically early aged 37 when a pistol he was cleaning discharged a bullet). The room is known today as the Whitehead Room. It is decorated in a late-medieval style, with a massive inglenook, huge chimneys and traceried windows. These are by Ernest Heasman (1874-1927), a local Sussex man and specialist in stained glass. There are about 35 of them and they depict variety in music and also a brief history of English music. There are copies of them in the Abbey archives which are just waiting for someone to describe and index them.

Whitehead's Music Room complete with organ.

The Music Room was intended for country house entertainment, singing, charades and games and was suitably furnished. There is a minstrels' gallery and the alcove in the far corner held a triple-manual (three keyboards) pipe organ. The massive fireplace is composed of Italian woodwork and red Siennese marble. The inglenook served as a warm corner in a room that was difficult to heat. Outside, high on the north-west corner of the Music Room, close to his carved stone monogram, Whitehead placed a beautiful stone statue of the muse of music complete with lute. A photograph taken prior to 1933 shows that this statue was damaged soon after being erected. However, when it was cleaned in 1993 and the broken arm restored, the date 1894 was discovered on the lute.

Muse of music statue on the exterior of the Whitehead Room

Robert Whitehead also built on the top of the hill north of the house an extensive and lavish range of farm buildings with a water tower over the entrance (now the clock tower). The architect is not known. High up on the western face of the tower can be seen Whitehead's initials, RW, together with a crowned lion, the words *In spe vivo* (I live in hope) and the date 1885. It is similar to the inscription on the south eastern gable of the house. The tower at the entrance to the farm housed a reservoir, which was fed from a spring in an artesian well at its south western corner. The well was investigated in 1996 by a local firm of bore hole engineers. They found it to be 1.8 metres in diameter, brick-lined and 30 metres deep with 18 metres of water in it. Old photographs from the time of Robert Whitehead show a windmill on the top of the tower for pumping the water up into it.

Documents in the Abbey's possession, dated about 1890 and which were probably drawn up in preparation for the sale of the property, include a map of the layout of the farm and the position of the drains. This ground plan of the farm shows it to be a very large rectangle within which were all the pens for the animals, including a bull pen; the various stores are smaller rectangles. The different areas were connected to each other by rails set into the ground to facilitate the transport of fodder and stores.

For various reasons Whitehead put the property on the market again in about 1891, but he loved Sussex and was finally buried beside the old Saxon church in Worth village. By the time he left he had extended the estate to about 2,000 acres of woods, farms and houses.

Lord Cowdray (1856-1927): The house in its heyday

Finally, in 1894, Paddockhurst was bought by Weetman Dickinson Pearson who, in 1910, received a peerage as the first Baron Cowdray. A Yorkshire man, Pearson had started with a firm of building contractors at Bradford and had worked on Dover Harbour and the first Blackwall Tunnel in London.

He began to look abroad for civil engineering contracts for the building of railways, dams, harbours and tunnels. His very successful business was to be supplemented later by the discovery of oil in Mexico. He was at the time a Member of Parliament but was so frequently absent from the House of Commons that he was referred to as "the Member for Mexico."

Beginning in 1895, Cowdray employed a well-known architect of the time, Sir Aston Webb (1849-1930), who was responsible for the facade of Buckingham Palace as we know it today.

Webb remodelled and embellished Whitehead's house. A third floor was added and an east wing along the line of the south front. A large Winter Garden with skittle alley extended the building further eastwards. There were enormous greenhouses growing tropical fruits. Particular attention was paid to laying out the gardens for the pleasure of weekend house parties. Unfortunately, few signs of these gardens now survive. Cowdray extended the estate to over 5,000 acres, most of which the family retained after the 1933 sale.

The inner gates were introduced by Lord Cowdray

Cowdray was created a Viscount in 1917 for his war work. After the First World War he set in motion new plans to develop the west front of the house of 1865 with its domestic buildings and stable block. Thus came into existence the long stone frontage that is seen today. The drive, with its metal drain covers bearing the name Paddockhurst, was straightened and the inner gates set up. In 1921 the tower on the hill was installed with a clock and eight bells in memory of Cowdray's youngest son Geoffrey, killed in 1914 at the Battle of the Marne.

The memorial clock tower, previously a water tower

Part II

A Look at the House

Front Hall and Banqueting Room

We begin our 'tour' at Reception in the front hall, which has a moulded ceiling. From the house's beginnings until the early 1920s the entrance was through the port-cochere, a drive-in porch which was spacious enough to enable guests arriving and departing to do so under cover. This explains the very wide space for the doorway and the presence of the two recumbent statues of 'Welcome' on the left and 'Farewell' on the right. In about 1921, the porte-cochere was replaced by the small porch still remaining.

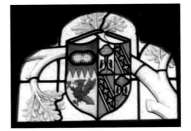

The stained glass windows in the front hall link the Cowdray coat of arms with those of various families connected by marriage with his family. These are, from the left (pictured top to bottom here), the Churchill, Knatchbull-Hugeson and Denman families. The window on the right is a memorial to Cowdray's deceased son Geoffrey.

Four of the stained glass windows

These links are reproduced again on the coloured ceiling of the Banqueting Room, entered through the double doors on the left of the front door, and in that room there is also an impressive stone carving over the fireplace of the Cowdray coat of arms. The coat of arms consists of a pair of suns over a gryphon (a fabulous creature with an eagle's head and wings and a lion's body) together with two supporters, a deep sea diver and a Mexican peasant. These latter figures recall Cowdray's engineering work in Dover Harbour and his oil interests in Mexico.

Lord Cowdray's coat of arms in the Banqueting Room

As we leave this room and proceed through the next doorway in the near corner to our left one can see the domestics' staircase with its solid granite steps and above it stained glass windows, which are the signs of the Zodiac. Worth School takes its cross and crown crest from another of these stained glass window designs.

The granite staircase

*Some of the stained glass
windows decorating the
domestic stairwell*

Retracing our steps, the double doors
on the far side of Reception open onto
the Inner Hall.

INNER HALL

The lower walls have panelling in this part of the house, the part for family and guests. The upper walls used to be covered in red damask. All the ceilings are moulded plaster.

Detail from the moulded ceiling in the Inner Hall

The glass in the windows recalls Lord Cowdray's official positions: High Steward and later Member of Parliament for Colchester, President of the Air Board, and Lord Rector of Aberdeen University.

The large window a little further along on our right is interesting. In the top row of panes, the eagle perched on a lotus leaf devouring a snake is the official symbol of Mexico. In the second row there are the dates 18-95 and on one side the initials WDP (Weetman Dickinson Pearson) while on the other side is AP (Annie Pearson), his wife.

Exiting through the door in the corner opposite the window leads to the Small Drawing Room.

Three of the Inner Hall windows

SMALL DRAWING ROOM

In this room, the fine ceiling is noteworthy and also the beautiful wooden panelling with, just beyond the entrance, the repeated pattern on the carved wooden 'column'. The empty space between the top of the panelling and the ceiling may have been intended to have a frieze as in the Cowdray Room. A signature found behind the hessian on the wall

Detail from the ceiling of the
Small Drawing Room

during renovations in 1992 dates the room to 1885, when Robert Whitehead was the owner. This room would have been a cosy place, which the family probably used when they were alone.

Leaving this room we enter the main stairwell and can see in the ceiling the words, "Welcome ever smiles". On the front of the large stone fireplace, with its beautiful carved cherub's face, we have yet again the Cowdray coat of arms. The grand staircase is believed to be Austrian pollard oak. The foliage design of the panels is very elaborate and suggests rococo models. Hidden underneath the stairs is a strong-room.

The rest of the house lying to the east is entirely the work of Sir Aston Webb. (A description of the rooms it contains follows below, but these rooms are not open to the public.)

Detail from the stone fireplace at the foot
of the main staircase

VESTIBULE, BILLIARD ROOM, WINTER GARDEN, DOMESTIC OFFICE AND CALEFACTORY

This Vestibule, now an office, has a very beautiful stone ceiling adorned with the signs of the Zodiac. It leads into the Billiard Room and the Winter Garden, both of which are now part of the monastic library.

The Billiard Room on the left is lit from a window in the ceiling, with the Cowdray coat of arms and his motto, "Do it with thy might." The wooden floor is inlaid with the outline of a billiard table and also carved rosettes. On one wall there is a glass showcase with an example of the carved pigskin with which the walls of the room used to be covered.

Detail from the glazing in the ceiling of the Billiard Room

The Domestic Office (now the monastery print room) still has over the fireplace a large stone slab, covered with the names of local country house families.

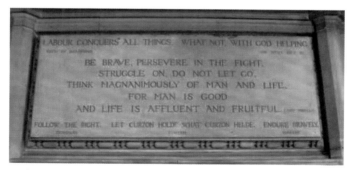

Family names recorded above the fireplace in the Domestic Office

Originally, the Winter Garden had a skittle alley down the middle and also a glass roof but now it is tiled. The Calefactory at the eastern end of the building is confined to the monks.

Resuming the tour, one returns via the Inner Hall to Reception. A single door in the corner to the right leads to the Cowdray Room. A glance through the window of the door on our left reveals the beautiful Victorian blue and white patterned tiling of the former kitchen passage.

The Victorian tiles of the kitchen passage

THE COWDRAY ROOM

This beautiful room has much that is noteworthy. The panelling and doors, with their finely wrought handles, are made of mahogany; likewise the sideboards. There is a minstrel's gallery, now curtained off. The plaster frieze, depicting the history of transport, is the work of Walter Crane (1845-1915), a very well-known illustrator and artist of the time. He executed the work in 1896 and a little tablet above right on one of the window panels records this fact. The Victorian pram in the farthest panel is remarkable; the panel is so narrow and yet there is perfect perspective. The cyclists in the centre panel between the windows are thought to be Lord and Lady Cowdray. The doors at the end lead into the former Winter Garden (see above).

Two images from Cowdray frieze

The East Wing and South Front

On exiting the Cowdray Room, notice in the area on the left the windows which are typically Victorian with smaller opaque shapes inserted into the larger panes. Going out onto the terrace by the door beside the window seat Aston Webb's wing of 1895 can be clearly seen. It is reckoned one of the finest pieces of work he did on the site. Beyond it lies the former Winter Garden. The terraces were created by Lord Cowdray and the magnificent view to the South Downs confirms the Victorians' choice of site. Before we leave this spot, we should notice the two projecting stone gargoyles up on the building to our right.

The first floor window over to the right was that of the Map Room, in which in 1944 the VIIIth Corps and other soldiers billeted here planned their part in D-Day and the invasion of Europe.

South front of the East wing

Following the terrace around one can see high up on the first gable a stone carving of the perched eagle devouring a snake, as in the Inner Hall. As one proceeds along the terrace, the windows on the right belong to former drawing rooms and at the top of each drain pipe can be seen the Cowdray gryphon holding in its talons the millstone from his crest.

One of the elaborate embellished drainpipes and
symbol of Mexico portrayed on the south gable

Beyond the porch, the building on the right is the Whitehead Room. Turning the corner and mounting the steps we enter the front quadrangle. Above head height in the new entrance to the Whitehead Room one can see six beautiful red and blue stained glass cherubs' faces just under the ceiling. Beyond the doorway, in the exterior wall, we can see close up Robert Whitehead's monogram with the date 1883 and above it on the pinnacle the beautiful Muse of music statue.

Robert Whitehead's monogram on the exterior of his Music Room

THE WEST FRONT

The front of the house as it is now appears more or less as Cowdray's architect, Aston Webb, intended except for the single storey wing on the north side. It is mock Tudor or late English Renaissance, exhibiting the characteristic gables and bay windows with tall, ornate brick chimneys. High up on the right hand second storey gable is Whitehead's crest and Latin motto and below it on the adjacent buildings are several stone gargoyles. The tops of the drainpipes in this area also have a rosette on them. On the left hand gable of the house the Cowdray coat of arms appears once again. The Mexican peasant in poncho and a deep-sea diver can also be clearly seen.

Lord Cowdray's coat of arms displayed on the front of the house

At the end of the building there is a tunnel entry into the back yard, but this was not the entry into the old stable block. That was bricked up and is no longer visible except at the back door on the other side of the building which has the date 1865. The great cedar tree to the left of the house was moved there on Cowdray's instructions, to break the line of the buildings and hide a tall boiler chimney; an indication of the trouble which he took over the site.

THE ENTRANCE PORCH

In its own way, the porch is also a thing of beauty. Surmounted by two large stone gryphons, each holding in its talons the millstone and the millrind or axle, in the centre is a viscount's coronet. The large brass handles of the front door form the shape of two interconnecting Cs. This could be identified as the union of Lord and Lady Cowdray, combining two Cs to form a loop of the door handle. The heavy oak door itself, with its Tudor style linen fold panels, is reminiscent of the Gothic / Scottish baronial style of the Victoria & Albert museum. Carved on the outer front door is the Cowdray coat of arms. The large door hinges are inlaid into the wooden structure of the door continuing the Tudor theme. The bolts that hold the heavy duty hinges carry the detail of the Tudor rose. Likewise, internally, the fixing nut for these bolts is beautifully detailed as another bud of a flower or indeed as a coronet, as can be seen in the Viscount's coat of arms.

The interior of the porch, also Aston Webb's work, has the four seasons of the year in coloured glass, one of which is signed by him with his personal symbol – a spider's web – and the date 1923.

Detail from the Winter window